Original title:
Friendship by Design

Author: Kaido Väinamäe
ISBN HARDBACK: 978-9916-89-094-3
ISBN PAPERBACK: 978-9916-89-095-0
ISBN EBOOK: 978-9916-89-096-7

Symphony of Shared Stories

In a world of whispers, tales unfold,
Echoes of laughter, memories bold.
Hearts intertwined, connected we stand,
Woven in stories, hand in hand.

From the mountains high to the valleys deep,
Dreams shared softly, secrets we keep.
Each voice a note in a grand design,
Together we weave a story divine.

Paths that we crossed, journeys we take,
In this grand symphony, bonds we make.
Notes of resilience, harmony bright,
Guiding us gently through the night.

A tapestry rich, colors collide,
Each thread a moment, none can hide.
With courage and love as our guiding star,
We find our home, no matter how far.

So let us gather, share in delight,
Fueling the fire, igniting the light.
In this symphony of lives intertwined,
A chorus of dreams, our souls aligned.

Cradled in Care

In warmth and comfort, we find our rest,
Gentle reminders, we are blessed.
Hands that nurture, hearts that share,
Wrapped in love, cradled in care.

Through storms of life, we stand as one,
Beneath the shadows, we find the sun.
Voices of solace, whispers so near,
In moments of doubt, we're always here.

Each smile a beacon, a light to embrace,
Finding our strength in this sacred space.
Together we flourish, together we grow,
In the garden of life, love's seeds we sow.

Like gentle raindrops on thirsty ground,
In every heartbeat, our hope is found.
With every tear, a new joy we bear,
Holding each other, cradled in care.

As the sun sets low and the stars appear,
We gather close, knowing no fear.
For in this embrace, we've learned to thrive,
Cradled in care, we keep love alive.

Heartstrings in Harmony

In twilight's soft embrace we find,
A melody that's intertwined.
With whispers low, the night shall sing,
Two hearts as one, the joy they bring.

Through laughter bright and tears that flow,
A gentle touch, a warm hello.
In every beat, the love does play,
Together strong, we find our way.

Beneath the stars, our dreams we weave,
In silence shared, we choose to believe.
For in this dance of fate we roam,
We've found a place to call our home.

Weaving Bonds

Threads of kindness, softly spun,
In every face, a tale begun.
With every smile, a bond is cast,
In simple moments, shadows pass.

Together we stand, side by side,
In joy and sorrow, we abide.
Through storms that rage, and skies so blue,
Our strength emerges, tried and true.

With hands entwined, we pave the way,
In unity, we find our stay.
A tapestry of dreams we sew,
In every heart, our love will grow.

The Tapestry of Togetherness

In every thread, a story told,
Of joys and hopes, both brave and bold.
With colors bright, we paint our tale,
Through valleys low and mountains pale.

Each stitch a moment, every hue,
Reflecting all that we pursue.
With love and laughter, we embark,
Together shining through the dark.

In woven paths, our spirits soar,
Each bond a treasure we adore.
For in this fabric, rich and rare,
We've found the beauty that we share.

Symphonies of Souls

In harmony, our spirits blend,
A symphony that won't just end.
With every note, we rise and fall,
A dance of joy that weaves through all.

Through trials faced and rivers crossed,
In every gain, there's never lost.
Together we find our perfect key,
In this sweet song, we feel so free.

With gentle whispers, we compose,
A melody that gently flows.
For in these tunes, our hearts unite,
In symphonies that light the night.

Touchstones of Togetherness

In laughter's glow, we find our way,
Hand in hand, through night and day.
Moments woven, thread by thread,
Together strong, where hearts are led.

Through storms we dance, in joy we stand,
With open hearts, we face the land.
Each whisper soft, a bond refined,
Touchstones cherished, intertwined.

In quiet times, our souls ignite,
Comfort found in shared delight.
With every step, we gently trace,
A tapestry of love and grace.

In sunlit hours, we bloom and grow,
Seedlings of trust, we plant and sow.
Through trials faced, united be,
Touchstones bright, for you and me.

The Sculpture of Shared Dreams

With every thought, we sculpt the night,
Carving wishes into the light.
Hands entwined, we shape our fate,
Pressing on, we navigate.

In visions bold, we chase the sky,
Chiseled hopes that never die.
Through every tear, we find the stone,
A masterpiece of love we've known.

With every laugh, we breathe the fire,
Molding passions, hearts inspired.
In silence deep, the dreams unfold,
A canvas bright, our stories told.

Together we, artisans at play,
Crafting memories with each day.
In twilight's hush, we find our way,
The sculpture stands, come what may.

Symmetry of Souls

In mirrored eyes, reflections gleam,
Two hearts entwined, a single dream.
The rhythm flows, a gentle tide,
In perfect balance, we abide.

Across the vast, we find our song,
A melody where we belong.
In harmony, our spirits soar,
A symmetry that we explore.

With every beat, a pulse divine,
In unity, our stars align.
Through whispered hopes, the world unfolds,
In every glance, a story told.

Together strong, we brave the night,
In each embrace, we find the light.
The universe, a grand design,
Symmetry of souls, so fine.

The Masterpiece of Memories

In every smile, a memory thrives,
Brushstrokes of love that come alive.
Colors blend in joyous hues,
A canvas deep with cherished views.

Through laughter loud, the moments stay,
A masterpiece that won't decay.
In quiet times, the echoes ring,
Each memory, a precious thing.

With open hearts, we paint the days,
Through light and shadow, love's soft gaze.
In every story, we build and weave,
A tapestry of dreams we leave.

With gentle hands, we hold the past,
An artwork fierce and ever cast.
In future's hands, we find our ways,
The masterpiece of memories stays.

Kinship in Artistry

In shadows cast by gentle light,
Two souls entwined, an endless flight.
With brushes dance, a timeless swirl,
Creating worlds, where dreams unfurl.

In laughter shared, their visions bloom,
From silence grows a vibrant room.
A canvas rich with stories spun,
A testament to all they've won.

With every stroke, a bond ignites,
In hues of joy and shared delights.
Together they weave, a tapestry,
Of memories held in harmony.

Through every challenge, side by side,
Art becomes their faithful guide.
In every shade, a whisper clear,
Their kinship grows, year after year.

Each masterpiece, a heartbeat's tune,
Underneath the silvery moon.
Connected souls, their spirits soar,
In artistry, forevermore.

Interlaced Echoes

Whispers bounce from heart to heart,
In every note, a tale, a part.
Fingers strum and voices blend,
Creating bonds that never end.

In melodies, the world they share,
With every rhythm, life's sweet care.
Harmonies like shadows play,
In night's embrace, they drift away.

Each echo holds a memory bright,
Reflecting warmth in the dead of night.
Unified in every sound,
In music's grace, their love is found.

Through chords and beats, they find their way,
In perfect sync, come what may.
Their laughter rings, a joyous cheer,
In interlaced echoes, ever near.

Together they dance, a swirling mist,
In every moment, none is missed.
With every song, their spirits weave,
In echoes shared, they both believe.

The Forge of Togetherness

In fire's glow, sparks start to fly,
Together they toil, both you and I.
With every hammer's sturdy strike,
We shape our dreams, and hope ignites.

Amidst the heat, our hearts unite,
Melting fears, igniting light.
In the forge, our visions merge,
Forging bonds that love shall surge.

As metal bends, so do we,
Chiseling life in harmony.
Each crafted piece, a story told,
Of resilience found in the bold.

Through trials faced and battles won,
The journey shared, our hearts as one.
In every creation, we find our place,
In the forge of love's warm embrace.

Together we rise, unyielding still,
With passion fierce and steadfast will.
In every blow, our spirits grow,
The forge of togetherness, a radiant glow.

Connections in Color

In vibrant hues, our spirits blend,
With every stroke, a message send.
The palette rich, our hearts align,
In connections formed, pure and divine.

A splash of red, a dash of blue,
In every shade, our love rings true.
Creating landscapes that intertwine,
In the vivid dance of space and time.

Colors whisper secrets bright,
Painting dreams that take to flight.
With every curve, our laughter flows,
In the warmth of joy, our art bestows.

From gentle pastels to bold embrace,
Our canvas tells of time and space.
In every layer, a story grows,
As connections deepen, the wonder shows.

Through art's own lens, we find our way,
In every shade, we chase the day.
In colored moments, forever we find,
The beauty of love, eternally entwined.

Crafting Memories

In the quiet of the night,
We gather simple things,
Laughter echoes softly,
Joy a song that sings.

With photos pinned to walls,
Moments come alive,
Each snapshot tells a tale,
In hearts, they thrive.

A cup of warmth we share,
Stories over tea,
Reminders of our past,
Bound eternally.

Time dances like a breeze,
Memories twirl and sway,
Each glance a gentle hug,
That never fades away.

We craft with hands and hearts,
A tapestry of love,
Woven tight with threads,
Sent from up above.

Weaving the Future

With threads of hope we stitch,
Dreams into the light,
A canvas pure and bright,
Ready for our flight.

Each plan a vibrant hue,
Each goal a sturdy knot,
Building paths ahead,
In this sacred spot.

With every choice we make,
We weave and intertwine,
A future shining clear,
That's ours, divine.

In shadows, we find strength,
In laughter, we find grace,
Crafting what's to come,
In this sacred space.

Together hand in hand,
We shape what's yet to be,
With love and trust as threads,
In our tapestry.

Threads of Connection

In the fabric of our lives,
Connections intertwine,
Each thread a gentle bond,
A tapestry divine.

With laughter in our hearts,
And kindness in our eyes,
We strengthen every link,
Under open skies.

In moments shared, we shine,
In struggle, meet our grace,
Through every twist and turn,
We find our rightful place.

Each story softly told,
A thread we hold so dear,
Connecting every soul,
With love that conquers fear.

In the dance of time,
We journey hand in hand,
Each thread a memory,
In this woven land.

Weaving Together Moments

Together we create,
A quilt of shared delight,
Each square a cherished memory,
Gathered in the light.

With every stitch we make,
We build our story true,
Moments woven softly,
In shades of me and you.

Through laughter and through tears,
Each piece finds its place,
A beautiful mosaic,
Of love's warm embrace.

In quiet, silent hours,
We gather all we find,
Each thread a whispered promise,
In hearts forever twined.

So let us weave with care,
Each moment rich and rare,
In the tapestry of life,
We find our treasures there.

The Interplay of Intentions

In shadows cast by dreams we weave,
Intentions dance, both bold and naive.
A tapestry of hopes, bright and wide,
Where whispers of the heart shall reside.

With every choice, a path unfolds,
In silence, the secret truth beholds.
The echoes of our wishes collide,
Creating a world where feelings abide.

Amidst the chaos, clarity gleams,
In the fabric of life, we stitch our dreams.
Together we forge through storms and sun,
The interplay of hearts can't be undone.

As stars align in cosmic embrace,
Intentions flourish, finding their place.
In the grand design, our souls entwine,
Each moment a masterpiece divine.

Boundless as the sky, rich as the sea,
In the dance of intentions, we are free.
With every breath, a story unfolds,
In the tapestry of life, our truth beholds.

Footprints in Harmony

In the sand where waves kiss the shore,
Footprints linger, stories of yore.
Each step a promise, soft, yet profound,
Whispers of the ocean's gentle sound.

As we walk, shadows align in peace,
In the rhythm of nature, our hearts find release.
The sun dips low, painting skies in gold,
Tales of connection quietly told.

Through valleys verdant and mountains high,
Footprints unite beneath the endless sky.
In the dance of the breeze, a melody sweet,
Harmony sings in the earth's heartbeat.

With every stride, the world starts to blend,
Footprints in harmony, journeying friend.
Together we wander, hand in hand,
Each mark on this path uniquely planned.

So let us create, as our spirits soar,
Footprints that echo forevermore.
In the canvas of life, bright and wide,
Harmony's song shall be our guide.

Harmony's Architecture

In the heart of the city, dreams arise,
Harmony's architecture fills the skies.
Each building a verse, each street a rhyme,
Crafting a tale that transcends time.

Windows wide open, letting light in,
Structures embracing where love can begin.
Corners that cradle, pathways that blend,
A symphony of spaces, a message to send.

Bridges unite, where differences fade,
Creating a haven, promises made.
With every corner turned, new visions call,
In harmony's haven, we find our all.

The arch of a doorway holds stories untold,
Of laughter and tears, the brave and the bold.
Each step a reminder of what we create,
In harmony's architecture, we elevate.

So let us build bridges, and reach for the stars,
Crafting a world without boundaries or bars.
In the framework of life, love is the key,
Harmony stands strong, forever free.

Kindred Spirits in Design

In sketches and lines, our spirits align,
Kindred designs, a bond so divine.
With every stroke, creation takes flight,
Crafting a canvas, day turns to night.

We weave through the colors of joy and despair,
In the fabric of friendship, together we dare.
Each hue a reflection of hearts intertwined,
In the art of connection, true souls defined.

As we navigate visions, hand in hand,
Building a world on which we stand.
Through trials and triumphs, we find the way,
Kindred spirits, come what may.

With passion ignited, we rise and create,
In the world of design, we find our fate.
Every pattern a story, every shape a song,
In the beauty of art, we effortlessly belong.

So let us paint, with strokes of the heart,
A masterpiece where kindness plays a part.
In the gallery of life, forever we shine,
Kindred spirits united, in design.

Forging Links in Time

In the quiet moments, we share,
Threads of laughter fill the air.
Time weaves stories, soft and bright,
Forging links that hold us tight.

Every glance, a gentle spark,
Lighting pathways, leaving marks.
Through the years, we grow and blend,
Forging bonds that never end.

In the shadows, memories play,
Reflecting on the dawn of day.
With each chapter, we refine,
The art of love, a grand design.

Carving time with every glance,
Fate doth lead us to this dance.
In the tapestry we find,
Forging links in heart and mind.

As seasons shift and moments flee,
Together, we etch our story.
Hand in hand through ebb and flow,
Forging links that ever grow.

Mosaic of Memories

Fragments scattered, shards of light,
Each a whisper of delight.
Colors vibrant, stories bold,
A mosaic, soon to unfold.

Pieces gathered, both old and new,
Each a part of me and you.
In this canvas, we define,
Life's sweet dance, a grand design.

Time may fade some, but not all,
In this frame, we stand tall.
Moments captured, forever bless,
A mosaic of our happiness.

Through the gaps, the light will seep,
Secrets shared, treasures deep.
In each fragment, love does shine,
Together we can intertwine.

As we build this masterpiece,
In every piece, our hearts increase.
Cherished echoes, we will find,
A mosaic of our hearts combined.

Sculpted Affections

In the hands of time, we carve,
Sculpted treasures we deserve.
With every touch, emotions flow,
Affections bloom, beautifully grow.

Chiseling hopes with dreams in mind,
Each stroke gentle, lovingly kind.
In the stone, the heart takes flight,
Sculpted forms in the fading light.

Whispers mold the essence true,
A masterpiece of me and you.
In this space, our souls entwine,
Each creation, a heart's design.

Through the dust of days gone by,
Sculpted love will never die.
With each moment, crafted fine,
Affection's art will brightly shine.

As shadows dance on passion's stage,
We etch our story, page by page.
In our hearts, the finest line,
Sculpted affections, ever divine.

The Art of Companionship

In every journey, side by side,
Companionship, our faithful guide.
Through storms and sunshine, we will tread,
The paths of life, where love is spread.

With laughter as our melody,
In silence, find sweet harmony.
In shared moments, trust will grow,
The art of love, forever flow.

Hands together, dreams we chase,
In every challenge, we embrace.
Through every turn, our hearts aligned,
In companionship, true love we find.

Whispers shared in the night's embrace,
Finding solace in your grace.
In each heartbeat, we are one,
The art of love, never undone.

Together weaving tales so grand,
Creating memories, hand in hand.
In the tapestry of life's design,
The art of companionship, truly divine.

The Architecture of Affection

In whispers soft, our dreams align,
With every touch, your heart is mine.
A sturdy bridge, in love we trust,
Built on the moments, strong and just.

Through windows wide, our joys expand,
In gentle light, we find our stand.
Each brick a story, love's sweet song,
In this structure, we both belong.

The walls embrace, no fear of night,
In shadows deep, your smile is light.
Foundations firm, our spirits soar,
In every heartbeat, wanting more.

As seasons change, our frames evolve,
In every challenge, we resolve.
Together here, we face the storm,
In love's design, we find our form.

So hand in hand, we'll build anew,
With every dream, our vision true.
An architecture of affection,
A lasting bond, our hearts' connection.

Sculpted Hearts

Chiseled edges, soft and raw,
In quiet warmth, our spirits thaw.
With gentle hands, we shape the clay,
A work of art that won't decay.

Fingers brush, the world stands still,
In every curve, I sense your will.
Hearts entwined, a masterpiece,
In love's embrace, we find our peace.

Through every flaw, we see the light,
For every shadow, love ignites.
With passion's fire, we carve our name,
In sculpted hearts, we feel the flame.

So let us mold, and let us bend,
In each creation, find a friend.
For in our hearts, the art is clear,
Sculpted softly, year by year.

Together here, with dreams so bright,
We'll shape our futures, chase the light.
With every touch, a story starts,
In every beat, our sculpted hearts.

Interlaced Journeys

Two paths converge, a winding road,
In every step, love's tale bestowed.
With open arms, we greet the bends,
In shared horizons, the journey blends.

Footprints soft on morning dew,
Each stride we take, a promise true.
In twilight's glow, our worlds entwine,
With every mile, your heart is mine.

Through peaks and valleys, we will roam,
In every journey, we find home.
With laughter bright and whispers low,
In love's embrace, we'll let it flow.

With stars as maps, we chase our dreams,
Through winding paths, in moonlit gleams.
Together here, we'll share our tales,
As interlaced as ships with sails.

So take my hand, let's explore new skies,
With every sunrise, love's sweet surprise.
In every detour, joy imparts,
On interlaced journeys, joined hearts.

Mosaic of Memories

In shattered glass, we find our face,
Every piece holds a warm embrace.
Together formed, in colors bright,
A mosaic spread by love's pure light.

In every shard, a moment stays,
Through laughter shared and gentle rays.
The cracks enrich, the stories flow,
In every hue, the love we sow.

Through storms we've weathered, joy we've found,
In quiet corners, our hearts rebound.
With every memory, sharp and clear,
In this mosaic, you are near.

So let us craft, with care and grace,
A tapestry of time and space.
In every piece, a thread of art,
A mosaic of memories, heart to heart.

Together we'll shine, a vibrant blend,
In laughter, love, and moments penned.
A work of art that's ever true,
In this mosaic, I find you.

The Grid of Together

In day's warm light, we weave and spin,
Through laughter's thread, our lives begin.
With every knot, our stories blend,
Together strong, we find our mend.

In storms we stand, side by side,
Our unity, a cherished pride.
Each joy and pain, a shared embrace,
In this vast grid, we find our place.

The strands we twist, the ties we bind,
In the darkest clouds, light we find.
Through winding paths, we journey forth,
With courage stitched, we chart our worth.

Through ebb and flow, the tides may change,
Our hearts align, though lives seem strange.
In silence shared, our souls take flight,
Bound by a love that shines so bright.

With every wish, we cast our hopes,
In harmony, we learn to cope.
Together, we are never lost,
In this grand grid, love is the cost.

Roots of Resilience

Beneath the soil, where whispers grow,
The strength of roots, they softly show.
In shadows deep, they anchor tight,
Unseen support, a quiet fight.

Through storms that rage and winds that tear,
These steadfast limbs, they do not scare.
With every challenge, they stand tall,
In unity, we rise through all.

Through droughts of doubt and floods of fear,
Our roots entwine, we draw them near.
In shared resolve, we learn to bend,
With every struggle, we ascend.

Each scar and mark, a tale to share,
Of how we've grown through pain and care.
In fertile ground, our spirits bloom,
Together strong, dispelling gloom.

With every season, we gain our might,
Against the dark, we find our light.
In the garden of hopes, we intertwine,
Roots of resilience, forever shine.

The Canvas of Companions

In colors bright, our dreams unfold,
A canvas shared, stories told.
With strokes of laughter, splashes of tears,
We paint our lives across the years.

Each hue a memory, rich and deep,
In vibrant shades, our secrets keep.
Through shadows cast, we find the form,
In this grand art, we weather the storm.

The brush of friendship, gentle and kind,
With every stroke, our hearts entwined.
A masterpiece, though rough in places,
In every flaw, love's truth embraces.

From somber greys to radiant golds,
In every passage, our tale unfolds.
Together we sketch, together we blend,
On this canvas, love knows no end.

With every finish, new starts await,
In timeless strokes, we navigate.
Through all creations, hand in hand,
The canvas of companions, forever stands.

A Colloquy of Hearts

In whispered tones, our stories flow,
Like rivers deep, with tales to show.
With gentle words, we bridge the space,
In this colloquy, we find our grace.

Around the fire, our voices rise,
Sharing dreams under starlit skies.
With every laugh, and every sigh,
In this exchange, our spirits fly.

The dance of thoughts, a graceful sway,
In heartfelt talks, we find our way.
Through shared silence, understanding blooms,
In trust and love, our friendship looms.

Each sentence crafted, a pledge to keep,
In the depths of night, our secrets seep.
Though words may fade, our hearts will hold,
The stories shared, a treasure untold.

With every chapter, we learn anew,
In this colloquy, the bond we grew.
Together we journey, hand in heart,
In this sacred space, we'll never part.

Crafted Cherished Chapters

In pages worn, stories unfold,
Whispers of dreams, both timid and bold.
With each word penned, a life takes flight,
Ink on the heart, in day and in night.

Moments captured in timeless embrace,
The laughter, the tears, each precious trace.
With memories stitched in the fabric of time,
A tapestry woven, a rhythm, a rhyme.

Through crafted lines, our truths we share,
In shadows and light, we lay ourselves bare.
Every chapter a step, a journey profound,
In the book of our lives, love's echoes resound.

From youth's bright dawn to twilight's grace,
The turning of pages, a slow, sacred pace.
With hope as our compass, we wander and roam,
In crafted cherished chapters, we find our true home.

So let us embrace what the future may yield,
With our hearts wide open, our stories revealed.
For each crafted chapter that we call our own,
Is a testament written, a legacy grown.

The Art of Embracing Differences

In colors diverse, our spirits unite,
With stories unique, we light up the night.
Each voice a melody, a song to behold,
In the dance of our differences, we are bold.

From various paths, we gather as one,
In laughter and kindness, our hearts weigh a ton.
For bridges we build on the shores of our soul,
The art of embracing makes fractured hearts whole.

With hands intertwined, we weave a new way,
In the garden of cultures, we cherish each sway.
The beauty of us, in each shade we blend,
In the art of embracing, we find a true friend.

Celebrate colors that paint our world bright,
In shades of compassion, we shine with delight.
For differences spark what's real and profound,
In the heartbeat of unity, love knows no bounds.

Together we rise, in harmony's embrace,
A symphony woven with grace and with pace.
In the art of embracing, we stand side by side,
With love as our canvas, our hearts open wide.

Canvas of the Heart

Upon this canvas, emotions take flight,
Brushstrokes of passion, a dance of pure light.
With colors that mingle, our stories unfold,
In the art of the heart, we find treasures untold.

Each hue a reflection, each shade a caress,
Whispers of yearning, the mess and the bless.
Caught in the moment, our spirits collide,
On this canvas of heart, love's secrets reside.

From the boldest of strokes to the softest of sighs,
We paint the horizons with dreams that arise.
In layers of feelings, our truths we expose,
The canvas of heart, where the wildflower grows.

With each heartbeat's rhythm, our colors align,
In the art of connection, our souls intertwine.
A masterpiece crafted with patience and care,
On this canvas of heart, we flourish and dare.

So let us create with the colors we find,
In the gallery of life, with love intertwined.
For the canvas of heart is where we belong,
In the brush of existence, we sing our song.

Gestures of Generosity

In little gestures, kindness takes form,
A smile, a hand, in the midst of the storm.
With hearts open wide, we share what we have,
In gestures of generosity, love's gentle salve.

From whispers of hope to the warms of embrace,
Each act a reminder of our shared space.
With the touched lives we change, the world starts to glow,
In the simple connections, love's river will flow.

In giving, we're gifted, a cycle so true,
As we share with each other, we find ourselves too.
In moments of laughter, in tears that we share,
In gestures of generosity, we show that we care.

For every small kindness, a ripple is sent,
An ocean of goodness, in our hearts, it is meant.
Through the fabric of life, in threads that we sew,
In gestures of generosity, we create and we grow.

With open arms, let us reach far and wide,
For the beauty of giving can never be denied.
In the spirit of love, let our actions impart,
The gestures of generosity, the song of the heart.

Alchemy of Souls

In shadows deep, we find our spark,
Transforming dark into the light.
With whispered dreams, our journeys start,
Entwined, we chase the stars at night.

Through ancient hands, our fates do weave,
A tapestry of heart and mind.
In every pulse, we learn to believe,
That love and magic are aligned.

In silent gardens, seeds are sown,
With gentle care, we watch them grow.
A bond unspoken, yet well-known,
In every glance, the feelings flow.

With every breath, the world transforms,
We grasp the essence, pure and true.
In swirling winds, our spirit warms,
A dance of souls in shades of blue.

When daylight fades, our hearts ignite,
With alchemy that time can't steal.
In unity, we greet the night,
For in this magic, we both heal.

The Palette of Us

Colors blend in soft embrace,
Each hue a story, rich and bright.
With every stroke, we find our place,
Together painting love's delight.

The canvas wide, our dreams take flight,
In splashes bold and whispers soft.
From shadows deep to beams of light,
We craft a world, so vast, aloft.

Each shade unique, yet intertwined,
In laughter's shade, in sorrow's gray.
With tender care, our hearts aligned,
In every moment, there we stay.

As seasons change, our palette shifts,
New colors born with each new day.
Through curves and lines, our spirit lifts,
In every hue, our love's display.

Together here, our art will bloom,
In vibrant strokes, our stories spun.
In joy and pain, through every room,
A masterpiece that's just begun.

Together in Time

Through ticking clocks, we walk as one,
In moments shared, our hearts align.
Each second passes, never done,
In every breath, a spark divine.

In whispered words, we trace our fate,
With each embrace, our bond is sealed.
A dance of laughter, never late,
In memories, our love revealed.

When shadows fall and daylight fades,
We hold the night, hands intertwined.
In silent moments, love cascades,
In timeless depths, our spirits find.

With every dawn, new tales unfold,
A journey shared across the years.
In stories written, brave and bold,
Together facing all our fears.

Through seasons' change, we bravely stand,
In heart and soul, we find our rhyme.
With every heartbeat, hand in hand,
Forever joined, together in time.

Sketches of Affection

With every line, our story grows,
In quiet whispers, love takes shape.
The strokes of kindness gently flow,
In every moment, hearts escape.

In shaded corners, secrets dwell,
A sketch of laughter, pure and free.
With strokes of grace, we weave our spell,
In ink and paper, you and me.

Through tangled thoughts and dreams once lost,
We find our way with every mark.
No matter what the price or cost,
In every trial, we leave a spark.

With tenderness, each canvas speaks,
Of afternoons wrapped up in sun.
In strokes so bold, our passion peaks,
In every heartbeat, we are one.

As art evolves, so does our bond,
In sketches drawn with love so true.
Together here, of dreams we're fond,
In every drawing, it's me and you.

The Canvas of Companionship

On a canvas bright with dreams,
Laughter paints the seams.
Shared colors blend and thrive,
In this space, we come alive.

With each brushstroke, hearts align,
In friendship, we find the divine.
Together, we shape our hopes,
Weaving through life's many slopes.

Our stories intertwine like thread,
In the warmth, no words need said.
Every memory, a vibrant hue,
A masterpiece made by me and you.

Through storms and calm, we stand true,
With open hearts, we see it through.
Every challenge we embrace,
Companionship's eternal grace.

As the canvas stretches wide,
On this journey, side by side.
Creating art within each day,
In the light of friendship, we play.

Blueprint of Bonds

In the sketches of our hearts,
Foundations built, never parts.
Each line drawn with care and might,
A testament of shared light.

Together we draft each dream,
In harmony, we plot the scheme.
With laughter echoing in the air,
Our blueprint sings of love and care.

Walls rise strong, yet flexible,
In moments of the inexplicable.
With every choice, a room we make,
Filled with memories, joys to take.

Through blueprints drawn in quiet nights,
We find solace in shared sights.
Hand in hand, we shape our fate,
In bonds, we find our perfect state.

Each corner holds a secret place,
Timeless stories, timeless grace.
The blueprint of us, a sacred find,
A tapestry of hearts entwined.

Crafted Souls in Harmony

In the forge of life, we meet,
Crafted souls in rhythmic beat.
With every touch, we shape and mold,
Creating stories yet untold.

Harmony sings, a gentle tune,
In moonlit nights, beneath the moon.
We dance along this winding path,
In unity, we find our math.

Hands entwined, we sculpt our days,
Each moment a masterpiece that sways.
With laughter echoing in the breeze,
Together we find our hearts at ease.

In the heat of trials, love's the flame,
In crafted souls, we find no shame.
Through every hammer, every strike,
We build a bond that feels so right.

As time unfolds our artistry,
In this craft, pure harmony.
Side by side, we stand as one,
In crafted souls, we've just begun.

Colors of Togetherness

In shades of joy and hues of care,
Togetherness is found everywhere.
Each color tells a tale anew,
In our palette, a vibrant view.

Golden sun and azure skies,
In each other's eyes, the prize.
With every brush, we leave a mark,
In the canvas where dreams spark.

Magenta laughter fills the air,
In this mix, we find our flair.
Colors blend in perfect sync,
In togetherness, we never sink.

Violet whispers, emerald dreams,
In every stitch, the heart redeems.
With each layer, we intertwine,
Creating paths that brightly shine.

Together we create the scene,
In the colors where we've been.
A tapestry of vibrant grace,
In togetherness, we've found our place.

Ties Woven in Shadows

In silence, whispers intertwine,
Secrets held, the heart's design.
Beneath the gaze of watchful night,
We weave our dreams in dimming light.

With every thread, a bond we sew,
In hidden places, feelings grow.
Through tangled paths and winding fate,
We find each other, never too late.

The darkness holds our laughter tight,
In shadows, we discover light.
Together, fears begin to fade,
As trust emerges, unafraid.

Each moment shared, a tale retold,
In the embrace of nights so bold.
Our spirits dance in whispered sounds,
In shadows deep, our love abounds.

Crafted Connections

Hands entwined, a gentle touch,
In shared moments, we build so much.
With every gaze, a story's spun,
Crafting bonds as bright as sun.

Through laughter shared, and tears we find,
The threads of life, so intertwined.
With whispered hopes and dreams aligned,
We sculpt our path, by fate designed.

In every word, intention flows,
A crafted bond that steadily grows.
Through storms we stand, through light we gleam,
Together, stronger, we dare to dream.

From distant shores to hearts so near,
We weave our stories, year by year.
In every heart, a place to stay,
In crafted connections, love finds its way.

The Architecture of Trust

Upon the foundation of open hearts,
We build a structure where kindness starts.
Each beam of faith, a solid guide,
In the architecture, we confide.

With every promise, a brick we lay,
Upon the walls, our fears give way.
Through laughter's echo and sorrow's sigh,
We fortify the bonds we rely.

In windows wide, transparency shines,
Letting in light, where love aligns.
Through storms and shadows, we will stand,
In the fortress built by heart and hand.

The rafters hold our hopes so high,
In every moment, we touch the sky.
With the architecture of trust in place,
A sanctuary where we find our grace.

Blueprints of Loyalty

With every line, a path we trace,
In blueprints drawn, we find our place.
Loyalty sketched with strokes sincere,
Through winding roads, we persevere.

In corners turned, our choices blend,
With every turn, our hearts defend.
In every challenge, strong we stand,
Together, we rise hand in hand.

Through trials faced and victories won,
We paint a future, brightly spun.
In loyal hearts, no fear resides,
Through every storm, our love abides.

The maps we draw, with care and pride,
Lead us into the light outside.
With blueprints of loyalty in view,
Together, we'll make dreams come true.

Inked in Affection

In the quiet dusk, whispers play,
Hearts intertwined in a gentle sway.
With every stroke, feelings ignite,
Inked in affection, love takes flight.

Captured moments, a canvas bright,
Brushstrokes of passion, pure delight.
Colors blend in a vivid dance,
Binding souls in a timeless romance.

Every line tells a story unique,
Silent confessions in shades mystique.
Bound by trust, through thick and thin,
Inked in affection, let love begin.

Through trials faced, hand in hand,
A masterpiece crafted, forever grand.
In each heartbeat, a promise true,
Inked in affection, me and you.

With every page turned, dreams unfold,
A tale of passion tenderly told.
Inked in our hearts, a vibrant hue,
Inked in affection, always anew.

Bonds Beyond Borders

Across the waters, beyond the skies,
A connection forged where truth lies.
Cultures merging, hearts so free,
Bonds beyond borders, you and me.

Different tongues, a shared embrace,
Unity found in every place.
Through laughter and tears, we find a way,
Bonds beyond borders, come what may.

With open arms, we greet the day,
Bridging the distance, come what may.
In every smile, a story shared,
Bonds beyond borders, love declared.

Hand in hand, we walk this land,
Different beats, but hearts ever grand.
Together we'll rise, together we'll stand,
Bonds beyond borders, love so planned.

From mountains high to valleys low,
The strength of friendship, a constant glow.
In every heartbeat, a melody sweet,
Bonds beyond borders, a rhythmic beat.

Streets of Shared Paths

In the city lights, our footsteps twine,
Walking these streets, your hand in mine.
With every corner, stories grow,
Streets of shared paths, love's gentle flow.

Echoes of laughter fill the air,
Moments cherished, a bond so rare.
Side by side, we carve our route,
Streets of shared paths, without a doubt.

Every turn brings a brand-new view,
Memories painted in every hue.
Together we wander, hearts aglow,
Streets of shared paths, forever go.

In the quiet evenings, stars align,
Guiding us home, your heart with mine.
Through ups and downs, let love grow,
Streets of shared paths, forever flow.

With every sunrise, new dreams ignite,
Hand in hand, we chase the light.
In the tapestry of life, we sew,
Streets of shared paths, love's greatest show.

The Framework of Unity

In the weaving of time, we find a thread,
Connecting our hearts, where hopes are fed.
In harmony's song, we stand side by side,
The framework of unity, our hearts open wide.

With every challenge, together we rise,
Building a structure that touches the skies.
In every heartbeat, a promise held dear,
The framework of unity, casting out fear.

In laughter and sorrow, we lay each brick,
Creating a fortress, sturdy and thick.
In every moment, a pledge we renew,
The framework of unity, strong and true.

Through storms that may come, we won't fall apart,
A bond that is forged from the depths of the heart.
With love as our guide, our journey is clear,
The framework of unity, forever near.

Together we stand on this solid ground,
In the framework of unity, strength can be found.
Hand in hand, we'll carve our own way,
The framework of unity, bright as the day.

Palette of Kindred Spirits

Colors blend in silent grace,
Each hue a story we embrace.
A canvas bright with shared delight,
Together, we ignite the night.

Brushes dance with gentle care,
In every stroke, a bond we share.
The palette blooms with every smile,
In friendship's hues, we walk a mile.

Each tone a memory to unfold,
A tapestry of hearts so bold.
Through laughter, tears, and whispered dreams,
We weave our lives, or so it seems.

The colors speak of who we are,
Guided by hope, like a shining star.
In this embrace, we find our art,
A masterpiece from every heart.

With every shade, our spirits soar,
A blend of lives forevermore.
In unity, we stand as one,
A palette bright beneath the sun.

Mended Hearts

From fractures deep, new love will rise,
Through gentle words and soft goodbyes.
We stitch the seams with threads of gold,
A tale of warmth and hope retold.

In quiet moments, healing grows,
A garden where affection flows.
We gather strength from scars we bear,
In mended hearts, there's love to share.

The past may linger, shadows cast,
Yet we embrace the love amassed.
With every sigh, we learn to cope,
In fragile hearts, we find our hope.

Together, we will face the dawn,
With tender bonds, the pain is gone.
Our laughter echoes, bright and clear,
In mended hearts, we've conquered fear.

So let us dance beneath the stars,
With joyful spirits, healed from scars.
Each heartbeat sings a song so true,
In love's embrace, we start anew.

Portraits of Understanding

With gentle eyes, we seek to see,
The hidden depths of you and me.
Each glance a bridge, each word a key,
In silent spaces, we are free.

Brush strokes of patience, love, and trust,
In every portrait, a bond robust.
We share the canvas of our lives,
Through joyful hues, our spirit thrives.

Each story painted, vivid, bold,
In every lane, the truth unfolds.
With open hearts, we dare to share,
The colors bright, the softness rare.

Together we sketch our dreams anew,
In every shade, a clearer view.
Through storms and tempests, we have learned,
In understanding, our hearts have turned.

So let us hang our art with pride,
A gallery where love resides.
In every portrait, we can find,
The beauty born of hearts entwined.

Echoes of Laughter

In every room where joy convenes,
Laughter dances, light and keen.
A melody that stirs the soul,
With every chuckle, we are whole.

Echoes ring through hall and street,
In bursts of glee, our hearts repeat.
A symphony of carefree days,
In laughter's arms, we find our ways.

The world may darken, shadows creep,
Yet joy is ours, a promise deep.
With every giggle, sorrow bends,
In joyful tunes, the heart defends.

So let us cherish all the light,
That paints our moments, pure delight.
In echoes sweet, our spirits climb,
In laughter's song, we lose all time.

Together, we will weave the thread,
Of joyous tales that must be said.
In every laugh, a bond we'll find,
In echoes bright, our hearts aligned.

Weaving Light in Shadows

In the dance of dusk and dawn,
Threads of gold begin to spawn.
Whispered tales in silken weave,
Echo dreams that we believe.

Fingers brush on twilight's seam,
Gathering glimmers, a soft beam.
With every stitch, a story glows,
In the heart where hope still flows.

Colors mingle, shadows play,
Crafting visions, bright and gay.
The canvas stretches, bold and free,
As light unveils what's meant to be.

Each thread pulled from quiet night,
Cradles warmth, ignites the light.
A tapestry of love and grace,
In the shadows, find your place.

So let us weave, with gentle hands,
A world where understanding stands.
In the fabric of the night,
We are artists, weaving light.

The Equation of Souls

In the realm where numbers blend,
Two paths meet, the journey penned.
Infinity in every glance,
A cosmic dance, a timeless chance.

Equations form in whispered sighs,
Two hearts beating, no need for lies.
An algebra of trust and fate,
Calculating love, never late.

With each heartbeat, a calculus grows,
Patterns emerge, the mystery flows.
X and Y in perfect sync,
In unity, our spirits drink.

Through the variables of life we roam,
Finding our way, we're never alone.
Solutions found in kindness shared,
The equation of the souls prepares.

So here we stand, hands intertwined,
Mathematics of the heart defined.
In every touch, the proof is clear,
Together we'll face what we hold dear.

Crafters of Joy

With gentle hands, they sculpt delight,
Creating worlds of purest light.
In laughter's echo, dreams take flight,
Crafters of joy, day and night.

From silver linings, they entwine,
A tapestry where hopes align.
In every smile, a spark ignites,
Painting life in vibrant sights.

They gather moments, tender and true,
Transforming gray to every hue.
In the heart's forge, they reshape fear,
With every tear, new joy draws near.

With every note, a symphony plays,
Harmonizing our tangled ways.
Through crafted dreams, we come alive,
In the joy of knowing we thrive.

So let us join, hand in hand,
As we weave this joyful strand.
Together we'll dance, create, employ,
In unison, we crafters of joy.

Symbiotic Colors

In the garden where colors bloom,
A vibrant dance, dispelling gloom.
Hues entwined in soft embrace,
Symbiotic life, a shared space.

The red of passion, the blue of peace,
Together they sing, their joys increase.
Golden rays lead the way,
In this palette, love holds sway.

Each shade whispers tales untold,
Of warmth, of courage, of hearts so bold.
They blend and swirl, in cosmic twirl,
In every brush, new colors unfurl.

In unity, they find their voice,
Together they rise, they rejoice.
Creating worlds in vibrant hues,
In symbiosis, they infuse.

So let us paint with hearts aglow,
In this spectrum, let love flow.
With every stroke, our stories blend,
Symbiotic colors, never end.

Threads of Unity

In a tapestry woven tight,
Different colors blend and merge,
Each thread holds a tale to write,
Together, we set the surge.

Hands reach out across the divide,
With warmth and kindness, we hold on,
In hearts, we cast our pride aside,
Together, we rise with the dawn.

Voices raised in harmony,
A chorus of strength we share,
In unity, we find the key,
To navigate our way with care.

Bonds grows deeper with each embrace,
A sacred space for love to grow,
In every challenge we must face,
Together, we shine and glow.

So let us weave our stories true,
With threads of hope that never break,
In every heart, a love anew,
A brighter world, together we'll make.

Colors of Camaraderie

In every shade, a friendship blooms,
Bright as the sun, soft as the night,
In laughter and joy, through life's many rooms,
Together, we paint with radiant light.

Through storms and sunshine, we stand as one,
Like a rainbow that spans the sky,
In moments of laughter, and battles won,
With colors of love, we fly high.

Each hue tells a story, richly spun,
From struggles faced, to joys we chase,
In life's vibrant dance, we all become,
The brush strokes of hope in this shared space.

We add to the canvas with every word,
Building a mural – bold and bright,
In every silence, and every unheard,
A symphony of souls in flight.

So let's celebrate this vibrant spree,
With colors of camaraderie in sight,
Together we'll rise, wild and free,
Creating a masterpiece of delight.

Whispers of Support

In the silence, a gentle breeze,
Carries whispers of love and care,
With every sigh, we aim to please,
Together, we find strength to share.

When shadows loom and hopes seem dim,
A soft presence stands near,
With every word, our worries trim,
In kindness, we wipe every tear.

Through storms we face, hand in hand,
Each heartbeat echoes a vow,
In trust, we firmly make our stand,
A bond unbreakable, here and now.

While the world may turn and sway,
We remain steadfast, hearts aligned,
In whispers of support, day by day,
A tapestry of love designed.

So let our voices blend like wind,
With tender words, we lift and soar,
In challenges faced, we will rescind,
For together, we are evermore.

Pathways in Parallel

On winding roads, our lives entwine,
Two journeys tracing a common path,
In every step, our hearts align,
Together, we conquer life's math.

Through valleys deep and mountains high,
We walk side by side, hand in hand,
With every laugh and whispered sigh,
In the beauty of dreams, we stand.

With every turn, our stories merge,
A symphony of hopes takes flight,
In unity, we face the surge,
Guided by stars that shine so bright.

In moments of challenge, we find grace,
Embracing the lessons life imparts,
With courage, together we'll face,
The winding roads that shape our hearts.

So here's to the paths we have crossed,
In harmony, let's chart our way,
In every journey, no love is lost,
Together, we rise, come what may.

Whispers in the Wind

Gentle breezes carry tales,
Of secrets held in shadows pale.
Leaves rustle softly, nature speaks,
A language known to those who seek.

Clouds drift by, a story spun,
As day gives way to setting sun.
Echoes linger, soft and bright,
In the calm of approaching night.

Winds of change, a haunting sigh,
Promising of what may lie nigh.
In the silence, hearts will dare,
To listen close, to feel the air.

Mountains stand as sentinels tall,
Guarding whispers that softly call.
Time wears on, yet still remains,
The essence of our hopes and pains.

So let us dance with fleeting breath,
Embrace each moment, conquer death.
For in the whispers, we will find,
The threads that bind us, love entwined.

Chiseled in Time

Granite stones and heartbeats blend,
Carved by nature, time a friend.
Each inch tells tales of what has been,
A history etched within the skin.

Rivers flow like inner thoughts,
Marking moments, battles fought.
With every wave, shores shift and fade,
Legacy of dreams once laid.

Footprints left on sandy shores,
Whispers echo, open doors.
In twilight's glow, shadows trace,
A journey long, a sacred space.

Time, a sculptor with gentle hands,
Carving visions from barren lands.
Each moment precious, each heart aligned,
In the canvas of life, beautifully designed.

Weaving threads of past and now,
In this tapestry, take a bow.
For in each story, we will find,
A reflection of the human mind.

Cartography of Companions

In the map of hearts, we wander wide,
Lines that twist, come close, divide.
Paths entwined through laughter and tears,
Marking moments through all the years.

Stars align in cosmic dance,
Guiding souls to take a chance.
Every face tells a different tale,
In this journey, we set sail.

Friendship's bond, a sacred thread,
Binding journeys where once we tread.
Through valleys deep and mountains high,
Together we laugh, together we cry.

Maps may fade, but love will last,
Charting futures, holding fast.
In every heartbeat, echoes found,
A legacy of love profound.

So we roam this world so vast,
With companions, shadows are cast.
For in our hearts lies the key,
A cartography of harmony.

The Play of Hearts

In the theater of dreams, we take our part,
A stage set bright for the play of hearts.
With each glance, our souls ignite,
A dance of passion in the fading light.

Scripted lines and whispered lore,
In the silence, we ask for more.
With every breath, we write anew,
In the gallery of the love we pursue.

Scenes change fast, emotions soar,
Yet in the chaos, we crave for more.
A glance, a touch, our hands align,
In this fleeting moment, we find the divine.

Curtains rise, and curtains fall,
Yet in our hearts, we answer the call.
For love transcends the bounds of time,
Forever etched, a perfect rhyme.

So let us play, forever young,
In the story of us, our hearts are sung.
As the final act comes to view,
Know this, my love, I cherish you.

The Alchemy of Us

In the quiet shadows, we blend,
Elements of laughter and tears,
Creating a bond that won't bend,
A potion brewed through the years.

Every glance a spark ignites,
With whispers of secrets untold,
Together we soar to new heights,
In this alchemy, we grow bold.

Fingers entwined like roots deep,
Nurturing dreams in the night,
In our hearts, we safely keep,
The promises made in twilight.

A dance of souls, we embrace,
Transforming the mundane to gold,
Through life's trials, we find grace,
Each chapter in our story told.

In the mixture of love and trust,
Forming a world that's all our own,
Amidst the chaos, we find rust,
And polish it to turn to stone.

Brushstrokes of Belonging

In a canvas wide and bright,
Colors blend, new shades arise,
Each stroke a tale of delight,
Binding hearts beneath the skies.

Together we paint our dreams,
With laughter echoing clear,
In every hue, a story beams,
Creating a bond sincere.

Through shadows and light we wander,
Finding shapes beneath the rain,
With each brush, we pause and ponder,
In this art, there's no more pain.

A masterpiece filled with hope,
With layers of joy intertwined,
In unity, together we cope,
In the beauty of us, we find.

With every splash, our spirits sing,
Harmony in colors free,
A home where love is the spring,
In brushstrokes of belonging, we're three.

Keys to the Heart

In whispers soft, secrets lie,
A treasure map within each soul,
With gentle turns, we learn to try,
To find the keys that make us whole.

With trust as the lock, we unlock,
Hidden chambers where love resides,
With patience, we weather the clock,
Each moment shared, the tide abides.

Through laughter and tears, we mold,
The promises forged in the night,
In light and in shadow, we hold,
The keys that fit just right.

A journey shared, hand in hand,
Each key a moment, a spark,
Together we stand, strong and grand,
Illuminating even the dark.

As doors open wide before us,
With every heartbeat, we start anew,
In life's gallery, we pour us,
Unlocking the dreams we pursue.

The Joy of Collaboration

In unity, our ideas bloom,
From diverse minds come forth the light,
Together we banish the gloom,
Creating wonders shining bright.

With every voice, a note we weave,
A symphony of sweet accord,
In shared visions, we believe,
Building bridges with each word.

The rhythm of teamwork flows strong,
Synchronizing hearts and hands,
Together we right the wrong,
In harmony, our passion stands.

Each challenge faced, a dance we learn,
With twists and turns, we innovate,
As flames of our spirits burn,
In collaboration, we create.

From sparks of thought, we ignite,
A fire of dreams that can't be tamed,
In togetherness, we find our might,
The joy of collaboration, unclaimed.

Choreographed Laughter

In the corner of the room, they sway,
Echoes of joy guiding their play.
Laughter dances like a gentle breeze,
Spreading smiles with effortless ease.

Every giggle a note in the song,
A melody of friendship, we all belong.
With each shared moment, they intertwine,
Creating a rhythm, a love so divine.

Beneath the moonlight, shadows prance,
Unity found in this joyful dance.
Together they leap, together they spin,
In the joy of the night, their hearts begin.

With every whisper, secrets unfold,
Stories of laughter and memories told.
A choreographed scene full of grace,
In the structure of joy, they find their place.

When the music fades and they breathe slow,
The laughter remains, a beautiful echo.
In the hearts of the friends who entwine,
Choreographed laughter, a bond so fine.

Tapestry of Trust

Threads woven tight, colors so bright,
In the fabric of friendship, they feel the light.
Each promise a stitch that holds them near,
Creating a tapestry free from fear.

With each gentle touch, they mend the seams,
Filling the gaps with hopes and dreams.
In the quiet moments, they find their voice,
In the warmth of connection, they rejoice.

A pattern unfolds with each shared story,
In the weave of their trust, they find their glory.
With hearts intertwined, they grow and bloom,
In the tapestry of life, there's always room.

Under the sun's embrace, they stand tall,
A patchwork of souls, together they call.
With every laughter, every tear,
The tapestry thrives, profound and clear.

Through the storms that may come, they stay strong,
In the threads of their trust, they all belong.
A masterpiece crafted by the hand of fate,
The tapestry of trust, a bond so great.

A Symphony of Support

In the orchestra of life, they play their part,
Notes of affection flow from the heart.
A helping hand, a shoulder to lean,
In the symphony of support, love is seen.

Each instrument adds to the harmonious tune,
Resonating under a warm, silver moon.
Together they rise, as one they stand,
Guiding each other with a steady hand.

Through crescendos of joy and soft sighs,
In the silence between, true friendship lies.
Every challenge faced, they face as a whole,
In the symphony's embrace, they find their soul.

With every challenge, their bonds grow tight,
In darkness and dawn, they shine so bright.
A chorus of voices, supporting the weak,
In the symphony of support, no one feels bleak.

So gather the players, tune up the strings,
In the orchestra of life, let freedom take wings.
For through the ups and downs, they shall always stay,
Creating a symphony that guides the way.

The Geometry of Kindness

In shapes and angles, kindness aligns,
Creating a pattern in the heart that shines.
With every gesture, a line intertwines,
In the geometry of kindness, love defines.

Circles of warmth that embrace the soul,
Learning from each other, they become whole.
Triangles of support, strong and true,
In the fabric of life, kindness breaks through.

With gentle equations, they find balance,
In the simplicity of a shared glance.
Every act a theorem, solid and sound,
In the geometry of kindness, connection is found.

In the corners of hearts, kindness resides,
Filling empty spaces where hope abides.
Each point connected, together they rise,
Building a world where compassion flies.

So let's draw the shapes with colors so bright,
In the canvas of life, let kindness ignite.
For in every angle, in every line,
The geometry of kindness forever will shine.

Mosaic of Moments

In twilight's embrace, we share a glance,
Reflecting dreams in a fleeting dance.
Each laugh is a thread, vibrant and bright,
Woven together in soft evening light.

Nature whispers secrets as night unfolds,
Stories of wonder, forever told.
With each heartbeat, a memory grows,
In a mosaic of moments, love beautifully flows.

From sunlit dawns to starlit skies,
Every heartbeat a promise, every sigh.
Fragments of life, each piece a delight,
Crafting a future from countless sparks of light.

In the tapestry woven by time's gentle hands,
We find our place in this vast expanse.
The colors of laughter, the hues of our fears,
Form the mosaic of memories through all of our years.

Together we journey, side by side,
In this vibrant story, there's nowhere to hide.
Each moment a jewel, each experience gold,
A mosaic of moments, together we mold.

The Canvas of Connection

With strokes of kindness, we paint our ties,
An infinite palette beneath open skies.
Each word a brushstroke, so vivid and true,
Creating a canvas of me and of you.

Through laughter and tears, our colors blend,
A masterpiece crafted, no need to pretend.
In shadows and light, our spirits entwine,
The canvas of connection, a love so divine.

With each gentle touch, new shades arise,
Exploring the depths where true beauty lies.
As seasons change, our colors may shift,
Yet the bond we cherish remains our greatest gift.

Moments like brushstrokes, each unique in form,
Blending into beauty within every storm.
Together we build, creating our fate,
On this canvas of connection, we patiently await.

In the gallery of life, our art on display,
A reflection of love in every way.
Through the years we'll stand, enjoying the view,
On this canvas of connection, forever, it's true.

Joint Ventures in Joy

In laughter's embrace, we chase the light,
Two hearts combined, everything feels right.
Each shared moment, a treasure we own,
Joint ventures in joy, where love has grown.

Through whispers of hope, we wander and roam,
Creating our stories, together at home.
In every adventure, a thrill we detect,
Joint ventures in joy, dreams we perfect.

With every sunrise, new paths we'll explore,
Hand in hand, seeking all we adore.
From quiet sunsets to wild, starlit nights,
Our joint venture in joy, soaring new heights.

Through challenges faced, we rise and revive,
In the warmth of your laughter, I truly thrive.
In this dance of life, we graciously twirl,
Joint ventures in joy, two souls in a swirl.

So here's to the moments, both simple and grand,
Together we'll journey, forever we'll stand.
In the book of our lives, let the pages unfold,
Joint ventures in joy, a love to behold.

Layers of Love

Beneath the surface, secrets reside,
Each layer revealing the hearts that collide.
Peeling back sorrow, revealing sweet grace,
In layers of love, we find our place.

Like petals of flowers, so soft yet so strong,
Each layer a note in our beautiful song.
Through trials we've faced, our bond only grew,
In layers of love, I cherish you.

With every heartbeat, new textures appear,
A tapestry woven from laughter and tears.
Together we build, with patience and care,
Exploring our layers, a journey we share.

From whispers of passion to echoes of trust,
In layers of love, it's forever a must.
Through seasons we flourish, in shadows and light,
Unraveling layers, our hearts feel so right.

So here's to each layer, a gift we unwrap,
A journey of love, with no need for a map.
Together forever, in life's simple dance,
In layers of love, we find our romance.

Touching Lives—Through Art

Brush strokes dance on canvas white,
Colors blend in soft twilight.
Each piece tells a hidden tale,
Whispering dreams where spirits sail.

In the gallery, hearts collide,
Footsteps echo, emotions glide.
A moment shared through painted sighs,
Art reveals the love that lies.

Fingers tracing ancient clay,
Sculptor's hands mold night and day.
With every curve and gentle line,
Artistry leaves the past behind.

Voices sing in vibrant hues,
Binding souls in what they choose.
Through every masterpiece we find,
Connection forged, and hearts aligned.

In the silence, meanings bloom,
Healing spirits from their gloom.
Art, a bridge to life anew,
Touching lives in all we do.

The Essence of Connectivity

Threads of laughter, woven tight,
In shared moments, pure delight.
A glance exchanged, a grin ignites,
Creating bonds that time excites.

In whispered conversations,
Find solace, joy, and aspirations.
Hands clasped together, warmth to share,
Through every challenge, love laid bare.

The pulse of hearts in harmony,
United rhythms set us free.
Distance fades within embrace,
In the essence, we find our place.

Through storms and trials, we stand tall,
Together we rise, never fall.
Stronger together, hand in hand,
In unity, we firmly stand.

With every story shared anew,
The essence of us shines through.
A tapestry of lives entwined,
In this connection, we are defined.

Fostering the Familiar

In the cozy glow of home,
Memories linger, never alone.
Each room whispers tales of old,
In laughter's warmth, our hearts unfold.

Traditions dance like autumn leaves,
Rooted deep, where love believes.
Gathered 'round the table's light,
Together, we create our night.

Familiar scents of meals prepared,
A testament to how we cared.
Echoes of voices, soft and dear,
In their presence, we have no fear.

Through seasons change, the bonds stay strong,
In this haven, we all belong.
Moments woven, stitched with love,
Fostering the familiar above.

From laughter shared to quiet sighs,
In every heart, this love applies.
In the familiar, we find our grace,
Cultivating warmth in every space.

The Sculptor's Embrace

Chisels chip in rhythmic grace,
Unearthing forms from time's embrace.
Stone reveals a hidden heart,
In each sculpture, a world apart.

With every strike, a dream awakes,
Creating beauty, as silence breaks.
The sculptor's vision, bold and true,
Molds lifelines into shapes anew.

Hands dipped in dust, a sacred art,
Translating passion, soul, and heart.
Crafting stories not yet told,
In the stillness, warmth unfolds.

Embracing flaws, the beauty thrives,
In every curve, the essence lives.
The sculptor's touch, a guiding hand,
Crafting love that understands.

With patience flowing from within,
Each form captures where we've been.
Through the sculptor's gaze, we trace,
Transformed by love, the sculptor's embrace.

The Fabric of Empathy

In quiet moments, understanding grows,
Threads of kindness in gentle flows.
Weaving hearts with every shared sigh,
A tapestry rich, reaching the sky.

Voices blend in a symphony sweet,
Each note a story, where souls meet.
Compassion blooms in the softest light,
Illuminating paths through the night.

With open minds, we bridge the divide,
Walking together, with arms open wide.
Stitching together our hopes and fears,
A fabric born from laughter and tears.

The warmth of connection weaves us as one,
Each thread a promise, a journey begun.
In the heart's embrace, we find our way,
Creating a masterpiece in each day.

In the loom of life, we find our place,
Threads intermingling, a gentle grace.
Together we flourish, together we stand,
In the fabric of empathy, hand in hand.

Harmonious Journeys

On winding roads, our spirits align,
Chasing horizons where dreams entwine.
Together we wander, hand in hand,
Exploring the wonders of this vast land.

The compass of friendship guides us near,
Every step forward, erasing fear.
Through mountains and valleys, the rivers flow,
In the heart of the journey, we truly grow.

With laughter as fuel and hope as our map,
We embrace the unknown, bridge every gap.
The melody of life whispers a song,
In harmony's cradle, we all belong.

Beneath starry skies, our dreams take flight,
Illuminating paths in the soft moonlight.
In the stillness of night, unity gleams,
Woven together through our shared dreams.

As seasons change and the years unfold,
Our stories blend, each chapter bold.
In this symphony of life, pure and true,
Every journey leads us back to you.

Heartfelt Collaborations

In the garden of ideas, we plant our seeds,
Nurturing visions, fulfilling our needs.
With open hearts, we gather and share,
Creating a space where love fills the air.

Hands reach out, intertwining with grace,
Together we build, a vibrant workplace.
With every effort, we strengthen our ties,
In the flow of creation, our spirit flies.

A chorus of voices, each distinct tune,
Harmonizing dreams under the same moon.
In collaboration's warmth, we find our way,
Painting our stories, come what may.

Through trials and triumphs, we stand as one,
Each task a treasure, a journey begun.
In the heart of teamwork, magic ignites,
Turning our hopes into dazzling sights.

As we celebrate moments, both big and small,
In this heartfelt collaboration, we rise, we fall.
Together, we flourish, together we inspire,
Fueled by the passion that never shall tire.

Interwoven Dreams

In the quiet corners of the night,
Dreams are woven in silver light.
We gather whispers, soft and clear,
In the tapestry of hopes, we hold dear.

With every heartbeat, visions ignite,
Colors of longing, shining bright.
A fusion of spirit, vibrant and free,
In the fabric of wishes, we find unity.

As stars align in the midnight sky,
We chase the currents where visions fly.
Through realms of wonder, together we soar,
With each thread woven, we seek even more.

In the embrace of the dreamer's plight,
Illuminating paths, guiding our flight.
The world is our canvas, vast and wide,
In the art of creation, we take pride.

In interwoven dreams, we hear the call,
A reminder that with love, we rise, we fall.
Together, we breathe life into our schemes,
Shaping our futures from infinite dreams.

Pillars of the Collective

United we stand, strong and tall,
Each voice a note in the symphonic call.
Together we rise, together we strive,
In the heart of the group, we truly thrive.

Bound by our dreams, we forge a way,
Embracing the night, we welcome the day.
With courage and grace, we build and create,
Pillars of hope, we overcome fate.

Each hand we lend, a story unfolds,
In whispers of trust, our future enfolds.
Together we nurture, together we dare,
The magic of unity blooms in the air.

In shadows and light, our spirits entwine,
With passion and joy, our destinies align.
For in every heartbeat, we share a song,
Pillars of strength where we all belong.

With laughter and tears, we journey as one,
In the warmth of the bond, we find our sun.
Together we harvest the fruits of the past,
In the pillars of the collective, forever we'll last.

The Artistry of Understanding

In strokes of kindness, we paint the scene,
With colors of thoughts, no space between.
Each voice a brush on the canvas of light,
The artistry blooms in the heart of the night.

We listen and learn, in stillness we grow,
With empathy's touch, we nurture the flow.
In conversations vivid, we dance in the fray,
The artistry of understanding leads the way.

With every shared glance, a masterpiece charts,
The harmony found in open hearts.
Together we cultivate a garden of grace,
Where differences mingle, embracing each space.

With tapestry woven from threads of our fears,
We craft our tomorrow through laughter and tears.
In this art of connection, we find a song,
The artistry of understanding makes us strong.

In the quiet moments, our spirits align,
Through strokes of compassion, our souls intertwine.
For in every encounter, a new dream begins,
The artistry of life, in each heart it spins.

Harmony in Diversity

In colors of wonder, we join hand in hand,
Each heartbeat a note in a wondrous band.
With rhythms united, we dance through the night,
Harmony in diversity, our shared delight.

From stories and journeys, we learn and we grow,
With respect as our anchor, together we flow.
The fabric of cultures, vibrant and bold,
In harmony's embrace, our tales are retold.

With voices all lifted, we sing of our pride,
In unity's chorus, we stand side by side.
Through laughter and joy, our spirits ignite,
For harmony thrives in every light.

In the depths of our hearts, we find common ground,
In the melody of life, our voices resound.
Each difference cherished, a treasure refined,
Harmony in diversity, beautifully aligned.

Together we flourish, a garden of souls,
In the symphony woven, our essence consoles.
With open hearts wide, we journey and find,
The beauty of harmony, forever entwined.

The Palette of Support

With colors of friendship, we paint the day,
In hues of compassion, we find our way.
Every stroke a promise, a brush of care,
The palette of support is vibrant and rare.

In shadows of doubt, we lend a hand,
With whispers of hope, together we stand.
In the warmth of our hearts, we sow seeds of light,
The palette of support shines brilliantly bright.

With laughter as gold and tears as our blue,
In every shared moment, we find something new.
With every challenge, we rise and we soar,
The palette of support opens every door.

With kind words as paints, we splash on the wall,
Creating a masterpiece, together we call.
In the journey of life, we color the way,
The palette of support here to stay.

In the gallery of dreams, our spirits unite,
In each canvas we craft, we create our light.
For with every layer, our bonds will sustain,
The palette of support, our love will remain.

The Design of Together

In the tapestry of time, we weave,
Threads of laughter, moments we believe.
Hand in hand, through every storm,
Together, we shape a love that's warm.

In shadows deep, we find the light,
Guiding each other through the night.
With every step, our dreams align,
In this dance, our hearts entwine.

A canvas bright, with hopes and fears,
We paint our path through joy and tears.
Each brushstroke tells a tale anew,
In the design, it's me and you.

With every heartbeat, stories unfold,
In the book of life, our love is told.
Whispers soft, in the morning dew,
In every moment, it's me and you.

So let us sail on this endless sea,
In the design of together, you and me.
Through all the chapters, we'll explore,
Hand in hand, forevermore.

Harmonies Handcrafted

In the symphony of days, we sing,
Each note a memory, our voices cling.
Crafted carefully, our hearts align,
In harmonies true, forever shine.

With rhythms soft, like whispered dreams,
We find our way through silver streams.
Melodies drift on the evening air,
In perfect cadence, we find our care.

Strings of laughter, echoes of light,
Dancing with joy, through day and night.
With every chord, our spirits rise,
In handcrafted love, no goodbyes.

Together we play this sweetest song,
In every moment where we belong.
With notes of hope in every refrain,
In harmonies crafted, we find no pain.

So let the music play on and on,
In the tapestry of love, we are drawn.
With every heartbeat, let's embrace,
In harmonies handcrafted, we find our place.

Notes of Nurture

In the garden of care, we sow the seeds,
Watering dreams, nurturing needs.
With gentle hands, we tend the vine,
In notes of nurture, our hearts combine.

Sunny days bring blossoms bright,
In the warmth of love, all feels right.
With patient hearts, we watch them grow,
In this sacred space, love's gentle flow.

Each petal soft, each leaf a song,
In the arms of nature, we belong.
Together we share in each sunrise,
In notes of nurture, our spirits rise.

With twilight's grace, we gather round,
In whispered hopes, our dreams are found.
Through every season, thick and thin,
In notes of nurture, we always win.

So let us cherish this sacred land,
With love as our guide, forever we stand.
In each heartbeat, let's softly pour,
In notes of nurture, we bloom evermore.

Strokes of Inspiration

With every brush, the colors blend,
On canvas wide, where dreams ascend.
Strokes of passion, bold and bright,
Inspiration dances, taking flight.

With gentle hues, the shadows play,
In the heart of art, we find our way.
Crafted with care, each line a kiss,
In strokes of inspiration, we find bliss.

Every splatter, a story told,
In every piece, a heart of gold.
Moments captured, fleeting and dear,
Inspiration whispers, always near.

Together we create, side by side,
In the gallery of life, there's nothing to hide.
With laughter and colors, let's unveil,
In strokes of inspiration, we shall sail.

So let us paint this world anew,
With love as our canvas, dreams in view.
With every heartbeat, we create the score,
In strokes of inspiration, forevermore.

Fractals of Faith

In shadows deep, belief does bloom,
A spiral dance in twilight's room.
Threads of hope weave stories bright,
In fractals' form, faith finds its light.

Each turn reveals a hidden grace,
A tapestry, our sacred space.
From chaos born, the patterns show,
In every heart, a seed to grow.

The mirror's edge reflects our dreams,
In every tear, a river streams.
Connections vast, we rise and fall,
In faith's embrace, we find our call.

The echoes whisper softly near,
Through labyrinths, we conquer fear.
In fractals of the soul, we find,
The strength to love, to be, unbind.

So trust the journey, seek the light,
Through fractals, faith ignites the night.
In every curve, a story born,
Together, we are never torn.

Patterns of Loyalty

In woven threads, our bonds entwine,
Through storms and sun, your heart is mine.
With each promise, loyalty grows,
In patterns rich, our love bestows.

Unbroken paths on winding roads,
Through heavy hearts and heavy loads.
Hand in hand, we stand so tall,
In patterns bright, we will not fall.

A silent vow in every glance,
Through life's dance, we take the chance.
As seasons change, our roots run deep,
In loyalty's embrace, we keep.

Through every trial, we rise anew,
In crazy storms, I stand by you.
With steadfast hearts, we blaze our way,
In patterns clear, we choose to stay.

So let the world throw what it may,
In loyalty, we find our way.
Through time's embrace and endless hue,
Our patterns dance, forever true.

Echoes of Empathy

In every heart, a story lies,
Whispers soft, like starlit skies.
We bridge the gaps with gentle grace,
In echoes deep, we find our place.

A silent nod, a knowing smile,
In shared moments, we walk a mile.
Through pain and joy, our spirits blend,
In empathy, we mend, we tend.

With open hearts, we breathe in pain,
In shared tears, we grow again.
Resonating warmth, a touch, a sound,
In echoes rich, our souls are found.

Through lives entwined, we build a bridge,
In every hardship, we find our edge.
Compassion's call, a tender thread,
In empathy, we move ahead.

So let us listen, let us care,
In echoes soft, we learn to share.
A world united, hearts set free,
In empathy, we come to be.

Design of the Heart

In quiet chambers, love does steer,
The design of heart, perfectly clear.
With every beat, a story spins,
In life's grand art, where love begins.

The brush of hope on canvas bright,
Strokes of joy, in morning light.
A tapestry of dreams we weave,
In design so fine, we dare believe.

Every scar a pattern bold,
In stories shared, our truth unfolds.
With pieces lost, we learn to mold,
In designs of heart, love's worth is gold.

Through every trial, the heart refines,
A blueprint drawn in love's own lines.
In shadows waning, light will chart,
The endless maze, the design of heart.

So let us dance to love's sweet tune,
In every phase, from night to noon.
With courage strong, we'll find our part,
In this wondrous design of heart.

The Fabric of Fellowship

In quiet corners, we weave our dreams,
Threads of laughter, stitched with care.
Hand in hand, we face the seams,
In every heartbeat, friendship's flare.

Through storms of doubt, we find our way,
Each knot holds strong, through trials we grow.
With whispered hopes, we greet the day,
In the fabric of fellowship, love we sow.

Around the fire, stories unfold,
Embers glow, memories ignite.
With every tale, our hearts are bold,
The warmth of kinship, our guiding light.

In moments shared, our spirits align,
Crafting bonds that time cannot sever.
Together we shine, like stars that twine,
In the fabric of fellowship, we are forever.

We cherish the laughter, embrace the tears,
A tapestry rich, adorned with grace.
Through the seasons, through all the years,
In fellowship's arms, we find our place.

Synthesis of Souls

Amidst the chaos, hearts collide,
An alchemy rare, we intertwine.
In each embrace, a truth confides,
A synthesis of souls, truly divine.

Through whispered dreams, we share the night,
With every glance, a pact is made.
Together we rise, in joy and fright,
In the dance of life, unafraid.

From different paths, we carve our way,
Each story adds to the greater whole.
In harmony, the shadows sway,
Creating a canvas for our souls.

With open hearts, we forge ahead,
An endless journey, side by side.
In every step, the fears we shed,
In the synthesis of souls, we confide.

Through life's tempest, we find our peace,
In laughter's echo, in silence deep.
In this union, our joys increase,
In the dance of souls, together we leap.

The Harmony of Convergence

Like rivers meeting in the twilight glow,
Our paths converge, a sacred space.
With every heartbeat, we come to know,
Together we form a vibrant trace.

In unity's chord, our voices blend,
A melody crafted from joy and strife.
With every note, we start to mend,
In the harmony of convergence, we find life.

Through winding roads and open skies,
We share our dreams, let courage soar.
In laughter's song, the spirit flies,
Together we gather, forevermore.

With hands held tight, we face the storm,
Every heartbeat a promise, a pledge.
In our togetherness, we find form,
In the harmony of convergence, we hedge.

From distant shores, we chart the course,
In every struggle, a dance of fate.
Bound by love's unyielding force,
In this harmony, we celebrate.

Echoes of Togetherness

In quiet whispers, love's anthem plays,
An echo of hearts, forever aligned.
Through laughter shared, and gentle gaze,
Together we tread, our paths entwined.

In the soft embrace of evening's light,
We find the strength to face the dawn.
With every hug, our worries take flight,
In the echoes of togetherness, we're reborn.

Through trials faced, we stand as one,
In moments fleeting, we find our song.
With every heartbeat, the race is run,
In togetherness, we all belong.

In shared reflections, we see the truth,
Mirrored souls, in harmony's grace.
In every challenge, we reclaim our youth,
In the echoes of togetherness, a warm embrace.

From wanderlust to quiet nights,
Our bonds strengthen, like roots of a tree.
In every moment, through all the fights,
In togetherness, we are truly free.

Milton Keynes UK
Ingram Content Group UK Ltd.
UKHW021208261024
450281UK00007B/101